Novalis

Zauber der Weisheit

Fotografien von
Klaus Ender

HERDER
Freiburg · Basel · Wien

Alles, was wir erfahren,
ist eine *Mitteilung.*
So ist die Welt in der Tat eine *Mitteilung* –
Offenbarung des Geistes.
Die Zeit ist nicht mehr,
wo der Geist Gottes verständlich war.
Der Sinn der Welt ist verloren gegangen.
Wir sind beim Buchstaben stehen geblieben.
Wir haben das Erscheinende
über den Erscheinungen verloren.

2:594

Es sind nicht die bunten Farben,
die lustigen Töne und die warme Luft,
die uns im Frühling so begeistern.
Es ist der stille weissagende Geist
unendlicher Hoffnungen ...

3:650

Wir sind
mit dem Unsichtbaren
näher als mit dem Sichtbaren
verbunden.

3:285

Mensch werden ist eine Kunst.

2:559

Wahre Mitteilung findet nur unter Gleichgesinnten, Gleichdenkenden statt.

2:559

Die Holzkohle und der Diamant
sind *ein* Stoff – und doch wie verschieden!
Sollte es nicht mit Mann und Frau
derselbe Fall sein?
Wir sind Tonerde,
und die Frauen sind Weltaugen und Saphire,
die ebenfalls aus Tonerde bestehen.

2:621

Könntest du nur sehen,
wie du mir erscheinst,
welches wunderbare Bild
deine Gestalt durchdringt
und mir überall entgegenleuchtet,
du würdest kein Alter fürchten …

1:288

Deine irdische Gestalt
ist nur ein Schatten dieses Bildes.
Die irdischen Kräfte ringen und quellen,
um es festzuhalten,
aber die Natur ist noch unreif;
das Bild ist ein ewiges Urbild,
ein Teil der unbekannten heiligen Welt.

1:288f

Die Liebe
ist der Endzweck
der Weltgeschichte –
das Eine des Universums.

3: 248

Was man liebt,
findet man überall und
sieht überall Ähnlichkeiten.
Je größer die Liebe,
desto weiter und mannigfaltiger
diese ähnliche Welt.

2: 485

Es gibt nur *einen* Tempel in der Welt,
und das ist der menschliche Körper.
Nichts ist heiliger als diese hohe Gestalt.
Das Bücken vor Menschen ist
eine Huldigung dieser Offenbarung im Fleisch.
Man berührt den Himmel,
wenn man einen Menschenleib betastet.

3:565

Bedürfnis nach Liebe
verrät schon eine vorhandene
Entzweiung in uns.
Bedürfnis verrät
immer Schwäche.

3:692

Ein Kind
ist eine sichtbar gewordne Liebe. –
Wir selbst sind
ein sichtbar gewordner Keim der Liebe
zwischen Natur
und Geist oder Kunst.

3:253

Das sind glückliche Leute,
die überall Gott vernehmen,
überall Gott finden;
diese Leute
sind eigentlich religiös.

3:286

Unter Menschen muss man *Gott* suchen.
In den menschlichen Begebenheiten,
in menschlichen Gedanken und Empfindungen
offenbart sich der Geist des Himmels
am hellsten.

3: 565

Das Ideal
einer vollkommnen Gesundheit
ist bloß wissenschaftlich interessant.
Krankheit gehört
zur Individualisierung.

3:681

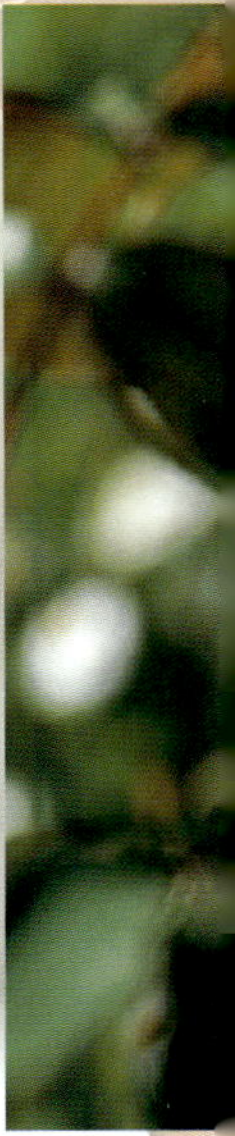

Je mehr man lernt,
nicht mehr in Augenblicken,
sondern in Jahren usw. zu leben,
desto edler wird man.
Die hastige Unruh,
das kleinliche Treiben des Geistes,
geht in große, ruhige, einfache und
vielumfassende Tätigkeit über,
und die herrliche Geduld findet sich ein.

3:686

Etwas zu lernen
ist ein sehr schöner Genuss –
und etwas wirklich zu können
ist die Quelle der Wohlbehaglichkeit.

3:575

Alle Zufälle unsers Lebens
sind Materialien,
aus denen wir machen können,
was wir wollen.
Wer viel Geist hat,
macht viel aus seinem Leben.

2:437

Das Herz
ist der Schlüssel
der Welt
und des Lebens.

2:606

Ist nicht jeder,
auch der verworrenste Traum,
eine sonderliche Erscheinung, die auch,
ohne noch an göttliche Schickung dabei zu denken,
ein bedeutender Riss
in dem geheimnisvollen Vorhang ist,
der mit tausend Falten
in unser Inneres hereinfällt …

1:198f

Alles Sichtbare
haftet am Unsichtbaren –
Das Hörbare am Unhörbaren –
Das Fühlen am Unfühlbaren.
Vielleicht das Denken
am Undenkbaren.

2:650

Der Sitz der Seele ist da,
wo sich Innenwelt und
Außenwelt berühren.
Wo sie sich durchdringen,
ist er in jedem Punkt
der Durchdringung.

2:419

Textauswahl aus: *Novalis Schriften. Das Werk Friedrich von Hardenbergs.*
Hrsg. von Paul Kluckhohn und Richard Samuel unter Mitarbeit von Heinz Ritter und Gerhard Schulz. Wissenschaftliche Buchgesellschaft, Darmstadt.
1 Erster Band: Das dichterische Werk, ^{3}1977.
2 Zweiter Band: Das philosophische Werk I, ^{2}1965.
3 Dritter Band: Das philosophische Werk II, ^{2}1968.
4 Vierter Band: Tagebücher, Briefwechsel, Zeitgenössische Zeugnisse, ^{2}1975.
Die Quellenangaben nennen den jeweiligen Band und die Seitenzahl.

www.herder.de
Gesamtgestaltung: Weiß – Grafik & Buchgestaltung, Freiburg
Repro: Skript Medientechnik, Freiburg
Herstellung: L.E.G.O. Olivotto S.p.A., Vicenza 2003
ISBN 3-451-28033-7

TO

ROSIE

LOVE FROM

....

Rosie dreamed of becoming an astronaut.

She loved rockets.
She knew more about the Moon than her teachers.
And she had collected loads of space toys.

But today Rosie had to think about making space rather than outer space. Her bedroom was so messy it looked like an asteroid had hit it.

Rosie carefully sorted through everything and began to fill her rucksack with old toys to take to the shed.

NASA

Rosie shuffled out of the house and down the garden path.

And there, resting on a pile of broken planks that used to be the shed, was a shiny metal rocket.

"Woah!" yelled Rosie.

"A SPACE ROCKET! IN MY GARDEN!"

Rosie charged up the ramp and clambered up a ladder to the control room. There was a chair in the centre, and she sat down and spun round and round.

As the chair turned she couldn't believe what she was seeing....

Flashing lights, blinking buttons and long levers surrounded her, and a small alien was hunched over, pulling at the controls.

"Err … hello?" said Rosie.

The alien turned round and yelped in surprise. He jumped backwards and sat down on the shiniest, reddest button Rosie had ever seen.

The doors slid shut with a *WHOOSH* and a *CLUNK*, and Rosie felt a rumbling that got bigger and bigger and louder and louder.

5 … 4 … 3 … 2 … 1 …

"Hold on tight!" the alien yelled. "We're off …"

LAUNCH
WHEERRPP!!

"... TO THE MOON!"

As they flew through space they quickly became best friends.

The alien told Rosie amazing stories about his travels through the galaxy, and how today he was heading to the dark side of the Moon. He was sure no one had ever explored it before.

The rocket touched down, and after finding a space suit for Rosie to wear they opened the door.

At the last moment Rosie ducked back inside, quickly tipped her rucksack out and pulled it on. Just in case.

"You never know, it may come in handy," she said.

Rosie and the alien bounced around, kicking up puffs of Moon dust and gazing out at the twinkling stars.

"Hang on," said Rosie, as she took a giant leap, "I think I can see ... tyre tracks?!"

"Maybe we're not the first to explore the dark side of the Moon after all," whispered the alien.

"Only one way to find out," replied Rosie.

"LET'S GO!"

They followed the tyre tracks around small craters and huge boulders until they came to the edge of a deep cave.

"What's that at the bottom?" wondered Rosie. The alien slowly lowered her down on the end of a rope, her footsteps echoing around the walls.

CLUMP CLUMP CLUMP CLUMP CLUMP CLUMP

"It looks like a metal glove." She stuffed it in her rucksack and quickly climbed back out.

"This will look great in my space-junk collection!" Rosie cheered.

Soon they came to a spooky Moon cave. The alien looked nervous as he peered into the gloom.

"Don't worry," said Rosie as she rummaged in her rucksack, "I've got my old wind-up rocket torch."

They crept into the vast cave and saw crystals covering every wall from top to bottom. As Rosie was gazing up at the sparkling rocks, she stubbed her toe on something and yelped loudly:

"OUCHYA!"

She knelt down to get a closer look: "Hmm, it's a small wheel."

Rosie stuffed it into her rucksack and they trudged up a narrow slope that led back to the surface.

They soon found themselves on the edge of a canyon. Rosie stared hard – she could see a mini satellite dish glinting on the other side.

"Well, we can't go around it," said the alien. "And I don't think we can jump that far, even with a run-up."

"I've got it!" yelled Rosie, as she gripped the valve on her air tank. "Grab my hand and hold tight."

WHOOOOOSH!

Rosie let out a sudden blast of air and they flew across the canyon, floating gently down on the other side.

"Awesome," she smiled. "I'm going to have the best space-treasure collection ever!"

Rosie was zipping up her rucksack when the alien tapped her on the shoulder.

She looked up and saw the tyre track leading to a huge boulder that had a ginormous shadow stretching out from behind it. The alien gasped:

"YIKES! RUN!"

"Don't worry," said Rosie. "Just stay very, very still...."

As they froze, a cute robot slowly wobbled out from behind the rock, blinking in surprise.

"Hello," smiled Rosie, "are you okay?"

"Hurrr-errr, not really," yawned the space robot. "I've been sleepwalking again and lost a few bits and pieces on the way."

He held out an arm which was missing a hand. He pointed to his leg which was missing a wheel, and then pointed to the side of his head which was missing a mini satellite dish. Rosie gasped.

"HANG ON!"

They carefully took the missing parts out of Rosie's rucksack one by one, while the space robot happily whirred and beeped.

Rosie and the alien helped repair their new friend, and soon the space robot looked his shiny best again.

Out of the corner of her eye Rosie could see Earth, and realised just how much she missed being there: "I think it's time to go home."

They said goodbye to the space robot and began their journey back to the rocket, following their own footsteps.

Over the canyon they went, back through the spooky Moon cave, and around the edge of the deep cave. Soon they were safely back in the control room of the rocket, ready to ...

BLAST OFF!

They slowly rumbled out of the sky into Rosie's garden. The door opened and she walked down the ramp and turned to wave goodbye to her new best friend one last time.

"Come back soon," yelled Rosie.

"I promise," said the alien.

Back in her bedroom, Rosie unzipped her rucksack and stared in surprise at the sparkling Moon rock the alien had left for her.

She gazed back up at the starry sky, hoping that her next BIG adventure would be out of this world.

GO DIVING?
Maybe I'll ...

HELP A DINOSAUR?

MEET SANTA?

Rosie, look out for more **Mini Adventures** books.
Go to www.orangutanbooks.com

Story by J.D. Green
Illustrated by Jo Lindley
Designed by Ryan Dunn

orangutan

First published by Orangutan Books in 2019
1 Queen Street, Bath BA1 1HE

www.orangutanbooks.com
Follow us @orangutanbooks

ISBN 978-1-83883-444-9

Printed in Italy
OB_PO201990

FSC
www.fsc.org
MIX
Paper from
responsible sources
FSC® C023419